SOME THOUGHTS ON THE INCARNATION

WITH A PREFATORY LETTER
TO THE ARCHBISHOP OF CANTERBURY

BY

J. ARMITAGE ROBINSON, D.D.

DEAN OF WESTMINSTER

NEW IMPRESSION

Wipf & Stock
PUBLISHERS
Eugene, Oregon

BY THE SAME AUTHOR.

SOME THOUGHTS ON INSPIRATION.

Crown 8vo. sewed, *6d.* net; cloth, *1s.* net.

SOME THOUGHTS ON THE ATHANASIAN CREED.

Crown 8vo. sewed, *6d.* net; cloth, *1s.* net.

THE STUDY OF THE GOSPELS.

Crown 8vo. *2s. 6d.* net.

LONGMANS, GREEN, & CO. 39 Paternoster Row,
LONDON, NEW YORK, AND BOMBAY.

Wipf and Stock Publishers
199 West 8th Avenue, Suite 3
Eugene, Oregon 97401

Some Thoughts on the Incarnation
By Robinson, J. Armitage
ISBN: 1-59244-508-X
Publication date 1/29/2004
Previously published by Longsmans, Green, and Co., 1905

DOMINO · ARCHIEPISCOPO · CANTVARIENSI

PRAESVLI · SAGACI · SVAVI · STRENVO

HOC · QVANTVLVMCVMQVE · PIGNVS · AMICITIAE

SVMMA · REVERENTIA

D · D

DECANVS · WESTMONASTERIENSIS

TO HIS GRACE

THE LORD ARCHBISHOP OF CANTERBURY

MY DEAR LORD ARCHBISHOP,

I welcome the opportunity of dedicating this little book to your Grace, as a token at once of sincere respect and of gratitude for personal kindnesses which can never be repaid. The three lectures here printed were given on the Saturday afternoons of last Advent from the pulpit of Westminster Abbey to a congregation which consisted largely of men. I was unwilling to publish them at the time, because, though they were the result of much study in the past, they were rapidly written and appeared to me to deserve no more than a passing report. I specially feared lest, if they appeared as a book, they might be regarded in some quarters as intended for a complete historical defence of the article of the Creed to which they chiefly refer. But the persistent cry of some of the clergy for an authoritative pronouncement of the Bishops of our Church, by way of meeting the questionings of recent times in regard to the Virgin-birth of our Lord, appears to me so greatly to mistake the temper of the questioners and to militate against the interests of sober enquiry, that I venture now to offer these lectures as an indication of the lines on which I think the subject may most advantageously be approached, and to preface them with a brief statement, addressed by permission to your Grace, in deprecation of the appeal for an official utterance of reasseveration.

No one will dispute the fact that in the minds of thoughtful men there is a very serious disquietude in regard to the doctrine of the Virgin-birth. It is only necessary to ask any doctor, any student of natural science, or any man who interests himself in scientific enquiries and their apparent conclusions, and endeavours to frame for himself a reasonable interpretation of the problems of life—to ask him not only what he himself thinks and feels, but what other men of his profession or class are saying to him, in order to discover that there is a real unsettlement of their minds in regard to a matter which hardly occurred to their fathers as a subject of enquiry. If we are to know how this grave disquietude is to be met, we must first understand what it is that is producing it. I think that there are two concurrent causes.

One is the spread of what would perhaps be called the scientific habit of mind. I mean more especially the temper which seeks everywhere for natural causes, and believes that they may yet be discovered where at present they are not obvious; which even when it will not deny the possibility of miracle is exceedingly jealous of what it regards as an unnecessary intervention of the miraculous. Many men of this temper can see the moral necessity of the miraculous in the case of our Lord's resurrection from the dead; but they cannot discover a like moral necessity for the Virgin-birth as the indispensable mode of the Incarnation. They are inclined to think that the union of God with Man might conceivably have been effected in some other way. They regard this particular miracle as accordingly making a demand upon their faith less reasonable than is made by any other miracle of the Gospel. Moreover, their professional or scientific training, or their scientific way of thinking, as they would put it, has absolutely disqualified them in their own judgment for any real belief in this miracle. These opinions spread far beyond the region in which they originate, and they constitute a genuine and widely-felt difficulty of belief, which deserves to be treated most sympathetically by Christian teachers.

Now, secondly, to men who live in this atmosphere there has come the knowledge that the belief from which they shrink has been called in question from another side. They are learning for the first time that it finds no direct expression in the writings of the two great teachers who above all others have expounded to us the doctrine of the Incarnation—St Paul and St John. They are, indeed, confronted by the first and third of our Gospels. But here they discover that criticism has been at work: that it tells us without ambiguity that the earliest *stratum* of the evangelic narrative contained no statement at all as to the mode of Christ's birth. They learn that careful and orthodox critics do not attach from the historical point of view the same weight to narratives peculiar to St Matthew as to other parts of the Gospels. They find themselves left with St Luke as the strongest historical evidence within the New Testament. They begin to wonder whether, after all, the tradition may not be an after-growth. They learn, too, that German scholars of the highest eminence have done what English scholars of the highest eminence in the same studies have not yet done—have definitely rejected the narratives of the Virgin-birth as in their judgment historically incredible. As the result of all this, they are confirmed in the position to which they had come on other grounds.

This is the situation, and these are the two principal causes. What ought to be the method to be pursued by the teaching office of the Church at such a moment? That is the question which profoundly interests us all.

In regard to the difficulty on the scientific side

little, I think, can be directly attempted. The intellectual temper of the age is beyond our control. The moment is one of peculiar interest: for the problem of the origins of life is being eagerly studied; and, though it is not our part to judge in a scientific controversy, it cannot be without interest to observe the admission in a very high quarter that the problem appears to be insoluble without some special intervention, which, whatever others may name it, we must speak of as the Hand of God. We welcome the indication, and wait in hope. Meanwhile we can urge upon such minds as I have been describing the meaning and the importance of the doctrine of the Incarnation as offering an interpretation of life, a philosophy of the whole of human history. We can explain the distinction in thought between the Incarnation and the special mode of its manifestation on the stage of our earthly life. If we can at all help men to realise the moral and intellectual necessity of the one doctrine, we may pass on with some hope to explain the unique appropriateness of the other.

On the critical side we can work, and are

working. The whole problem of the Gospels is being dealt with by the scholars of the Church in a way which promises the best results. There is a keen interest in it which is widely felt. The atmosphere is at present calm. Passions have not been aroused as they were by Old Testament criticism, and extravagance in consequence is comparatively rare. We are being trusted by the Church, and we recognise the responsibility which that trust brings with it. This quiet confidence is, I believe, the strongest testimony which the Church can at this moment offer to the whole class of minds which I have described.

Now, what is the new departure which in certain quarters is being urged upon us, and what will be its effect? We are asked to meet the disquietude of men's minds by appealing for a pronouncement from the episcopate to the effect that the Virgin-birth is a cardinal doctrine of the Christian faith. This pronouncement is, I gather, to take one of two forms. Either it is to be a formal reassertion of the truth of the Virgin-birth on the highest ecclesiastical authority, a statement that our Bishops really believe what we say twice a day in our Creed; or it is to be such a reassertion accompanied with a summary of the main arguments on which that article of the Creed rests.

What will be the effect of the first method on minds such as I have described? It will be regarded as an attempt to close the door of enquiry by the hand of authority. That, I take it, few of us would desire. It is utterly alien to the spirit of the English Church. It is a fundamental principle that criticism must be met by criticism, not by counter-assertion. We shall inevitably give the impression that we are using in despair our last available weapon. We shall thereby create a greater anxiety than that which we seek to allay.

What will be the effect of the second method? I believe that it will be still more disastrous. The argument for the Virgin-birth cannot be presented in a summary form without suggesting that it is far weaker than in reality it is. If the Bishops should quote, for example—and I have heard the suggestion made—the testimony of St Ignatius, they would at once raise the question,

Why do they not quote his great masters, St Paul and St John? If they make a summary defence, they will set up a target at which many a shaft will be aimed. For this will fairly be accounted the statement of the Church's case. It will be examined as such, and pronounced wholly inadequate as an argument for so astonishing a miracle.

If what I have said be at all grounded in reason, it follows that nothing can be more untimely than an appeal from the clergy to their Bishops to make at this moment an authoritative assertion that the doctrine of the Virgin-birth is a cardinal doctrine of the Christian faith. I might indeed take objection to the loose employment of the term 'cardinal doctrine' in such a connexion. If the Bishops were asked to declare that the Incarnation is a cardinal doctrine of the faith, such a statement would be superfluous indeed, but it would be true. But to say that the historical fact of the Virgin-birth is a cardinal doctrine of the faith is to use language which no Synod of Bishops, so far as I am aware, has ever ventured to use. It is to confuse the

Incarnation with the special mode of the Incarnation in a way for which Christian theology offers no precedent. But I let the point of phraseology pass: for it is the act of reassertion by authority of that which is questioned by criticism which I deprecate. Such an act is bound to produce an injurious effect upon enquiring minds. And it is likely to stir afresh the public discussion of a subject which does not gain by being publicly discussed.

There is a natural reserve of the English mind which has saved us hitherto from the interminable and most painful canvassing of this question which has gone on elsewhere. I believe that almost all of us desire that the subject should drop out of the arena of publicly canvassed questions. A pronouncement of the Bishops would only push it to the front again. It is quite another thing that some of the theologians amongst them should take natural opportunities of presenting the argument in a way that may reach doubtful minds. Some of them have done so already. But can any one believe that, to offer a single example, the signature of the Bishop of Worcester to a joint episcopal declaration on this matter could effect anything at all for perplexed enquirers in comparison with the writings of Charles Gore?

Briefly, then, I would say: At the present moment anxiety is rife, but open discussion is rare. The action urged either would seem to stifle enquiry by invoking authority, or would challenge disputation by offering a summary of arguments. There is anxiety, but we need not manufacture a crisis, we need not fall into panic. There is a true way of meeting this doubt. Our scholars and theologians are quietly taking it. I would implore the Church not to hamper and prejudice their earnest labours by interposing an utterance of authority which will rouse intellectual resentment and will not allay disquiet.

Your Grace will pardon me if I have written with needless urgency on a matter in which I might be confident that I should have your hearty sympathy. But when voices of alarm are raised, it is sometimes important that an expression should be given to the view of those who, while no less eager to maintain the truth, are opposed to alarmist action.

I remain,

Your Grace's sincerely devoted servant,

J. Armitage Robinson.

Westminster Abbey,
Ascension Day, 1903.

SOME THOUGHTS

ON

THE INCARNATION

I

The season of Advent is intended by the Church as a preparation for the great festival of Christmas. Christmas brings joys peculiar to itself. It brings the re-union of families; it calls on the middle-aged and the old to forget their years, and give themselves up to join in the pleasures of the little children. It calls the world to generosity and peace: it invites the rich to share their substance with the poor, and the injured or aggrieved to lay aside their resentment and seek reconciliation. It is a joyous time of innocent mirth and bountiful good will. It is the festival of the Holy Child, who was born to be the Prince of Peace.

Yet Christmas has its shadows for many of us as the years go on. It brings sad memories ot happy gatherings for ever past, and vacant chairs that can never be filled. It reminds us how far we have travelled on the path of life, and how distant are the voices of our own childhood. All this may have its compensations indeed for those who with a strong faith look forward joyously towards the eternal future. But to many a man Christmas itself brings a fresh sense of haunting doubts as to the security of his belief in the very truth to which Christmas is intended to witness. Easter presents less difficulty to his mind than Christmas. From the earnest contemplation of the Passion, he is led on by a kind of necessity to believe that such a life and such a death must have been followed by a resurrection, if the power of goodness to triumph over evil was to be manifested to the world. But Christmas seems to offer a more incredible and a quite needless miracle. He feels the beauty of the Gospel story, but he finds himself, year by year, further removed from any serious belief in it. He would like to enter heart and soul into the religious as well as the social side of the Christmas festival: he dares not stay away and let his children go to church alone: but the Christmas hymns are no longer real to him, he feels as though the foundations of his faith were undermined, and in the midst of others' joy he is perplexed and sad.

It is such men as this that I have had in my thoughts in planning this short course of Advent lectures. The Church must have a message to give to them, if she is to continue to assert, as she has from the beginning asserted, that her faith is in accord with the highest reason. It may not indeed be possible to remove the whole of the difficulty that they experience: for the spiritual world is not wholly to be interpreted in terms of the world of sense, and again and again our faith leads us up towards a region of insoluble mystery. But I believe that it is possible to propose some thoughts on the Incarnation which may help such men as I have spoken of to understand that the Christian belief is not at this point so unreasonable as at first sight, and without enquiry, it appears to them to be.

My design is a simple and an unpretending one. I shall try to state in plain words what we mean when we speak of the doctrine of the Incarnation, and why we attach so great importance to this doctrine. I do not propose to examine the philosophical foundations of the doctrine, or to trace the history of its development, or to justify the safeguards by which it was found necessary in early times to protect it from misconception. These are fascinating enquiries: they are among the highest tasks of the Church's theologians. They are also tasks most necessary to be undertaken: for the Church is bound in every age to give an answer concerning the faith she holds which shall correspond with the best thought and the most advanced knowledge of the age. But they require a special gift and a special training. Even to understand where the true difficulties lie, and to judge of the solutions which are proposed, demands no ordinary measure of intellect as well as a long course of patient preparation.

My present task is a humbler one. I wish to set out in terms which any thoughtful man who will take reasonable trouble can understand, first, what we mean by the Incarnation; secondly, what led up to it and made it possible; then, how as a matter of historical fact it was realised on the stage of the world; and lastly, what are its chief lessons and its most important issues.

First, then, what do we mean by the Incarnation? Let us begin with the word itself. It is a Latin word, to which no one English word exactly corresponds, and therefore we have borrowed it and made it our own. The root *carn-* means 'flesh.' Incarnate means embodied, or more strictly 'made to be in flesh.' The Incarnation signifies the coming of the Son of God in human flesh. The word 'incarnate' is well explained for us in our Nicene Creed in the words: 'Who for us men . . . was incarnate . . . and was made man.'

Here then is the doctrine of the Incarnation. In the language of the Gospel, 'The Word was made flesh and dwelt among us.' In the words of the Creed, 'The only begotten Son of God . . . very God . . . by whom all things were made . . . for us men . . . came down from heaven, and was incarnate . . . and was made man.'

Let us be clear about this at the outset. What we are now speaking of is the doctrine of the Incarnation: not the method by which the Incarnation was realised or manifested in human life. Let us keep to the order that we have laid down. What the Incarnation in itself is, that is the first question. In what way the Incarnation was brought about is a different question: and we shall gain much in clearness of thought if we take the first question first.

It is not unnecessary to insist upon this point of distinction. A man came to me not long ago, and said that he wanted advice as to how to help a friend of his who had great difficulty in believing in the Incarnation. I said: 'Do you mean the Incarnation itself—the fact that the Son of God became man for our sakes? or do you mean the mode of the Incarnation—the miracle of the Virgin-birth?' 'Of course,' he said, 'I mean the Virgin-birth.'

This confusion of thought is what I want to clear up at the outset. I do not myself see how a man who does not believe the Incarnation—that the Son of God was made man—can be expected to believe the miraculous birth of the Incarnate. If he cannot say in his Creed: 'Who came down from heaven, and was incarnate,' he cannot go on to add: 'By the Holy Ghost, of the Virgin Mary.'

I do not for a moment say that the two things can be separated: but I say that they can be distinguished and ought to be distinguished in our thought upon the subject. We must keep the true order of thought, if we are to arrive at a reasonable presentation of the faith.

It is from neglect of this principle of distinction that there are many men found to say offhand: 'I am asked to believe in a thing which my special knowledge of physiology together with my general scientific training has rendered me incapable of believing. Tell me of the noble character of Christ, tell me of His unrivalled self-sacrifice, and I will join you in the most loyal admiration. Indeed I have tried however distantly to follow Him, and His cross fills me with shame whenever I look upon it: it is at once the condemnation and the inspiration of my life. But the Incarnation—no. It has been credible in the past, but to-day it is credible no longer. We must reconstruct our beliefs, and cease to demand the impossible.'

May I speak just to such men for a moment, and not to the full believer in the Christian Creed, who finds nothing impossible or too hard for God? I would say: Make the distinction in thought to which I have referred. Leave, for the time being, the question of the mode of the Incarnation in the background, and consider only the doctrine of the Incarnation—that the

Son of God took human flesh, was incarnate and was made man. If you can once get reasonably clear about that, you can come on later to the consideration of the mode in which the Incarnation was divinely brought about. If you are convinced that an incarnation of God in human flesh actually took place, then and then only can you approach the evidence for the scriptural narratives and the Church's belief as to the mode of it with a mind that is open to the possibility ot its acceptance. If the Son of God was made man in the birth of Jesus, that was an event absolutely unique, utterly miraculous. If you find that to be a belief which is justified, as explaining what is otherwise inexplicable, and as giving the key to the mystery of human life; then you have reached a point at which you will be free to ask further whether, the event being unique and miraculous in itself, the mode of its manifestation may not conceivably have been unique and miraculous also.

I propose then to invite you, first of all, to consider the doctrine of the Incarnation in itself, apart from the question of the miraculous method of its realisation. If I am challenged for allowing this distinction, even in thought, I must reply that I have the highest authority on my side. The two greatest exponents of the truth of the Incarnation, and of its world-issues, are St Paul and St John. Though we have no right to conclude from their silence that they held any other belief than that of our first and third evangelists, yet their extant writings do not, as a matter of fact, tell us anything of the miraculous birth. I draw no conclusion from their silence but this: that we are justified in speaking of the Incarnation itself by itself, and without introducing at the moment the question of the particular mode in which it was realised in history.

I have made a long introduction: but it was absolutely necessary to do something to clear the ground in order to enable what I believe to be a large class of minds to approach the consideration of the Incarnation with a free and unfettered judgment. In the short time which is still at our disposal this afternoon, I shall enquire to what extent the revelation of God and of man's relation to God, which was made to the Jewish people, prepared the way for the doctrine of the Incarnation, the manifestation of God in human flesh.

I ask you to consider that great first lesson about God and man which is taught at the opening of the book of Genesis. It does not matter for our purpose who wrote that chapter, or whether he was adopting more ancient materials, or was describing a kind of vision, or composing a kind of prose-poem. All I want you to observe is the spiritual lesson which he was enforcing—a lesson which lifts this particular account of Creation high above all the cosmogonies anywhere to be found in ancient literature.

His purpose is to explain the relation of man on the one side to the animals and the inanimate creation below him, and on the other side to God above him. He writes with no scientific knowledge, but with the wisdom of a true observer of nature, as it presented itself to his eyes and mind. He begins with God: 'In the beginning God . . . .' All that is, is from God. But it is from God in due order, in an ascending scale, beginning with darkness and chaos, and passing gradually into light and harmony. This conception is profoundly scientific, and it is worked out in detail according to the most accurate observation possible at the time.

First comes inanimate nature: earth and water; sun, moon, and stars. Then comes vegetation; then various forms of animal life, fishes and birds and beasts; and last of all comes man. The general idea is wholly in harmony with our latest scientific thought. The details may be slightly out of order here and there: but the conception is that which we now speak of as evolution—a ladder of being, rising step by step from the lowest to the highest. The stages are marked off somewhat conventionally by adopting as a framework the days of the week—six days of work in which new developments are observable, and a day of rest in which no such vast changes are to be traced. This is merely the literary setting of the thought, and need not detain us. Yet in passing we may note one feature which is surprising. If any of us were to attempt for ourselves to arrange the various steps in the development according to the days of the week, we should almost certainly keep one day all to itself for the ultimate stage of the appearance of man. Not so the Hebrew seer: he puts the higher animals and man together on the sixth day, not fearing in the least to suggest the intimate connexion between man and the animals which come next beneath him. On the bodily side of his nature man is but little removed from the animals, though even in this respect he stands at the head of all. His true distinction is of another kind: it is a spiritual distinction, which is described in the words: 'the image and likeness of God.' Man is made in God's image. He is set at the head of creation as God's visible representative. He is to rule as God's vicegerent. 'Let them have dominion' is the charter of his authority. Man is the link between nature and God.

What nobler conception of human life has ever been offered in any literature, than is given in this simple picturesque parable of the world's beginnings? It is in a chapter like this that we *feel* inspiration, even if we cannot define it. We are sure that it was the Divine Spirit who taught this early writer the sublime lesson which is embodied here.

His first and immediate purpose may have been to lift the Jewish people high above the nature-worships of surrounding nations—the Chaldean worship of the heavenly bodies, and the Egyptian worship of sacred animals. But I am now concerned to show that this teaching is the intellectual and moral preparation for the doctrine of the Incarnation. The story of the human race declares how sadly man failed to realise this great ideal: how, instead of reigning as God's visible representative on earth, he sought to be independent of God: how he sinned against the order in which he was placed, and chose to follow his own will, instead of the Divine will: how he degraded his human nature from its likeness to the Divine.

Had man not thus failed, we can conceive that by the education of the Divine Spirit, the image of God would have been more and more clearly manifested in the steady progress of the race; until at last the Incarnation of the Son of God as man might have crowned the whole history, and the perfect man would have manifested the perfect image of God.

But we have to do with a world in which man as a fact has failed: has fallen short of his own human nature and its proper destiny. In the midst of this failure, and with a view to its ultimate remedy, God taught one nation in plain terms that human nature is essentially God-like, that it is capable of presenting the very image and likeness of the Divine.

This, then, is the great first lesson which we must never let go. There is something in man which is naturally akin to God. In virtue of that, man is in some sense at least God's child. Human nature is a fit medium for the visible manifestation of the Divine. The way is open for the Incarnation, the union of God and man, the appearance on this earthly scene of one who is both perfect God and perfect Man, who is the express image of the Divine, who can truly say: 'He that hath seen Me, hath seen the Father.'

I am deeply conscious that this is but an imperfect statement of what has been nobly called 'The Gospel of Creation.' There are doubtless other ways of setting forth the natural capacity of man for the manifestation of God, which might appeal with greater force to more philosophic minds. But I feel that my best hope of helping you is to present the matter in the way in which I am myself accustomed to conceive of it. And what I may call the naturalness of the Incarnation, as the reasonable sequel to the revelation of God and man which was taught to the mind of the Jewish people, has always seemed most helpful to me. It is for this reason that I commend it to you to study and work out for yourselves.

But I must rapidly conclude. I have been

able to dwell on one element only—though, perhaps, the most important element—of the preparation of the Jewish people, and through them of the world, for the Incarnation. I should have wished to go much further in this department of the subject, and to show how God taught the Jewish people by their history, first, that Israel was in a special sense the son of God ; and, secondly, that Israel should one day be summed up and represented in a single person who should crown her history and bring in the kingdom of God.

That little people to whom God was so near witnessed, as no other people has witnessed, to the instinctive belief of humanity in its Divine origin and its glorious destiny : uttered as no other people has ever uttered the instinctive cry of humanity for a Deliverer, who should of necessity be Divine as well as human.

But all this I must pass by, with a mere mention to show that I have not forgotten its importance; and in my next lecture I must endeavour to consider the historical manifestation of the Incarnation on the stage of a sinful human world.

II

In our first lecture we considered the meaning of the word Incarnation. We saw that it meant 'embodiment,' or, more strictly, 'coming to be in flesh': and that it was used as a brief summary of the truth expressed in St John's Gospel by the statement 'The Word was made flesh and dwelt among us'; the truth declared in the Creed that the eternal Son of God 'came down from heaven . . . and was made man.' I specially invited you to draw a clear distinction in thought between the doctrine of the Incarnation itself and the particular mode in which the Incarnation was realised in history; and to examine the first of these matters in the first place apart from the second. We then passed on to show that in the fundamental teaching of the Old Testament there was a preparation for the doctrine of the Incarnation. For the Old Testament teaching about man is tha he stands at the head of the Creation, as being made 'in the image of God': that is to say, that human nature is by its constitution capable to some extent of manifesting God; that it is a fit medium for the incarnation of the Divine: whence it follows, that there is nothing inherently inconceivable in the union of God and man.

I did not enter upon the philosophical justification of this teaching. I merely called your attention to it as an actual teaching by which Israel (and the world through Israel) was being prepared for the Incarnation. The Fatherhood of God to man is not expressly declared in the Old Testament: but a certain kinship between God and man is suggested, so that in time God came to be spoken of as 'a Father unto Israel,' and Israel came to think of itself as 'the Son of God.' Similarly, the coming Incarnation of the Son of God is not expressly declared in the Old Testament; but the fundamental relation of human nature to the Divine is so taught as to pave the way for what was to follow, and to prepare earnest Jewish thinkers like St Paul and St John to understand and interpret the Incarnation when it came.

It is an inevitable disadvantage of a short

course of lectures on so great a subject, that thoughts can only be thrown out, and cannot be followed up and justified in detail; and also that difficulties which suggest themselves to the hearers' minds must be passed over without notice. There is one difficulty, however, which readily arises, and which, as a matter of fact, has been pressed upon me by a correspondent who heard the first lecture: and on this I should wish to say a few words.

I may state it in my own language as follows. An early observer of nature and of man may reasonably have regarded man as vastly superior to all else in the world, and so nearly akin to God as to be a worthy object of the Divine favour in the highest degree: and an earlier age than our own may have found no special difficulty in believing that God should unite Himself with man, the foremost of His creatures, for whose sake Creation itself appeared to have been originated and wrought out. But the whole tendency of modern scientific enquiry has been to depress the relative value of man. Is it then equally reasonable to hold these beliefs to-day, when the telescope has revealed myriads of other worlds, and our earth has dwindled to an inconsiderable speck? When we reflect on the littleness of man, as modern science has declared it to us in a hundred ways, are we any longer justified in regarding humanity as of such importance, as so central to the universe, as to call for an incarnation of the Divine in human flesh?

This is a real difficulty. How much it cost the greatest of our modern poets is known to students of the *In Memoriam.* The immensity of the universe oppressed Tennyson like a nightmare. He felt it as only a poet could, and a poet of our time in full sympathy with the advancing studies of natural science. But, to use his own words spoken of another:

> He fought his doubts and gather'd strength,
> He would not make his judgment blind,
> He faced the spectres of the mind
> And laid them: thus he came at length
> To find a stronger faith his own.

But the difficulty is not a new one, though it has received a new emphasis. It was a Jewish poet, with the teaching of Genesis full in his mind, who wrote in the eighth Psalm:

> When I consider Thy heavens, the work of Thy fingers;
> The moon and the stars, which Thou hast ordained:
> What is man, that Thou art mindful of him?
> And the son of man, that Thou visitest him?

The distance between God and man was infinite then: it is neither more nor less to-day. For the fuller revelation of the physical insignificance of man has been counterbalanced by the fuller revelation of his intellectual and moral greatness. The mind that takes in so much is greater than the material universe which it takes in. And the greatness of moral character has come to be recognised as the true human distinction, and as a ground of superiority which is not affected by any disclosure of man's physical insignificance.

The wonder remains exactly the same. The condescension of God is infinite. The reasonableness of this condescension depends on factors in the problem which are to us unknown. This earth may be but a stage on which a drama is being enacted which beings of another order may be observing to their eternal profit. So at least thought St Paul when he wrote in the Epistle to the Ephesians, that 'to the principalities and powers in the heavenly region' there was being 'made known through the Church the very varied wisdom of God.'

It requires after all an act of faith—and not an act of reason by itself—to say 'He came down from heaven, and was incarnate, and was made man.' Faith, I say: and I mean faith in the condescension of God, faith in the essential kinship of man to God; faith in a Shepherd who seeks one sheep of a hundred until He finds it, faith in a Father who cannot forget that He has a prodigal son. It comes after all to this: that we believe in a love which is beyond our understanding:

For the love of God is larger
  Than the measures of man's mind:
And the Heart of the Eternal
  Is most wonderfully kind.

I pass on now to offer some thoughts on the historical manifestation of the Incarnation as it is taught us in the New Testament.

Our earliest Gospel is St Mark's. We shall do well to ask in what form he depicts the incarnate life of the Son of God. He begins where the first disciples of our Lord began. He begins with the self-manifestation of Christ to the people at large. While John the Baptist is preaching his mission of repentance, Jesus, now thirty years old, suddenly comes on the scene. He fulfils the sign which John had given: 'a stronger than I am is coming after me.' He presents Himself as 'a prophet, mighty in word and in deed.' At the very outset He promises to fulfil all hopes, declaring that the long looked for time is come. He turns all eyes towards Himself. He heals the sick, He raises the dead. He proclaims that a new power is at work in the world—a little seed only as yet, but a seed that must certainly grow. He calls men to follow Him. He demands that they shall devote themselves to Him utterly and at any cost: the dearest earthly ties, even life itself, must be sacrificed for His sake. His demands, like His promises, are such as no man had ever made, or ever had the shadow of a right to make. He aroused an indescribable enthusiasm in the simple folk of Galilee, and the deadliest hatred in the envious and hypocritical leaders of Judaism. He was hunted to death, and crucified in Jerusalem. It was an unexampled tragedy. But it did not end there. It had an unexampled sequel. On the third day His tomb was empty, and an angel said that He was risen from the dead.

That, in the briefest outline, is St Mark's picture of the incarnate life of the Son of God. It derives its astonishing force from its simple realism. The language is bare and rude; it is often brief to obscurity. The wonder and the beauty lie in the facts. The brilliant light and the deep shade belong not to the art of the narrator, but to the events which he allows to speak for themselves.

As we read the story we ask ourselves: If indeed the Son of God 'came down from heaven and was made man,' can we conceive that His incarnate life could have been other than this which is here described? Must He not have lived so? Must He not have worked and spoken so? Must He not have suffered so? Must He not have risen so? Is it not all essentially appropriate? Can we conceive of a more appropriate life? Can we think of another issue? Must He not have displayed the new power in miraculous acts of helpfulness and restoration? Must He not have been crushed at last by human sin, if He refused to use that power to save Himself? Must He not, when the worst was undergone, have shown that the new power was stronger than death itself?

There is the picture. The existence of the picture is a fact. Account for the existence of the picture otherwise if you can. The simplest account, and to my mind the only intelligible account that can be given, is that the doctrine of the Incarnation of the Son of God is true: that 'the only-begotten Son of God for us men came down from heaven, and was incarnate, and was made man; suffered, and was buried, and the third day rose again.'

The picture is like nothing else: it is admittedly unique. It has filled the world with new ideas. It has taught us that character is the supreme measure of worth. It has taught us that self-sacrifice for others is the ground and basis of the highest character. It has changed our whole estimate of what is failure and what is success in human life. It has secured to us that which was an insecure guess before, the hope of immortality beyond the grave. It has secured to us above all the certainty that God loves us. In itself, and in its effects upon the world, the picture is unique. What imagination could have drawn it, if it does not correspond to facts?

And, mark you, the whole story is full of surprises. It is never what the people expect. It is not a natural product of the Galilean fishermen's minds. The people were astonished at the teaching which it records. At every miracle they were beyond measure amazed.

And it is full of miracle. And the miracle is always appropriate, though never anticipated. For if it was to be shown that a new power had come into human life, then the miracles are appropriate: for they manifest that new power as surmounting all obstacles, and repairing all losses, and supplying all needs, and bringing life everywhere in place of death. And the resurrection, the crowning miracle, is indispensable. 'He saved others, Himself He cannot save' was a truer taunt than they who flung it knew. Self-sacrifice for others must know no bounds: the cross was a Divine necessity in a world of sin. But goodness cannot in the final issue be defeated by sin; otherwise our human hope is blotted out; and so 'God raised Him from the dead.' The picture is full of miracle; but the miracle is demanded by the uniqueness of the situation.

This is the incarnate life which I would have you study first. Go to it again and again when problems beset you. Open your mind to the influences of that simple story. Again and again you will rise from the reading of it with a fresh conviction that it tells you of One who came down from heaven and was incarnate and was made man; who, in other words, by a voluntary act of self-limitation stepped out as it were of the invisible world and accepted the limitations of time and space for our sakes, taking our manhood upon Himself: of One who as man has conquered sin and death, and has lifted our humanity into union with God.

My brothers, if I have carried you with me thus far, then and only then can I hope to be of any help to you as we approach the peculiar miracle which attended the birth of Him who was at once God and man: who was, in the words of the ancient Christian hymn, 'God, of the substance of the Father, begotten before all worlds; and Man, of the substance of His Mother, born in the world: perfect God, and perfect Man.'

I shall not attempt to offer any naturalistic explanation of the facts recorded in the Gospels. I quite agree that in many so-called miracles what once seemed miraculous has ceased to seem miraculous, because a hidden law has come into sight which offers an unexpected explanation. A man would be bold who should deny that all miracles may some day be seen to be only results of higher laws which are at present hidden from our imperfect knowledge. But at present the

Gospel miracles are all miracles for me. Except, perhaps, in the case of the demoniac cures, I cannot see that any advance has been firmly made towards what would be called a natural explanation. But my faith is not staggered by miracles in a life which is altogether unique, and which I believe to be the Incarnation of the Divine. My reason asks that the miracle shall not appear to be a needless miracle; that it shall serve a worthy purpose; that it shall be in harmony with my whole conception of the incarnate life. If such it be, then I am prepared to weigh the historical evidence for it with a mind undisturbed by any desire to get rid of the miraculous element.

Can you go with me thus far? If so, let me ask: If a wholly new departure in human history was being made, is it unreasonable to suppose that this departure might be marked by a signal miracle? If miracle is ever in place as a witness to the intervention of a new power, challenging our attention and manifesting the 'finger of God,' was not the coming of the Son of God in human flesh a fit occasion for miracle? If a Divine life was entering into our weakened and death-stricken humanity, can we think it inappropriate that from the outset this life should manifest its power to transcend the natural order by which we are limited?

Believing as I do that the eternal Son of God, by whom all things were made, in the fulfilment of the eternal Father's will 'came down from heaven' (that is to say, came out of the unseen world) and clothed Himself with flesh, uniting Himself to our manhood, I am ready to believe that so unique an event might fitly be ushered in by the unique miracle of a Virgin-birth.

I am not asking now whether it was so, for that is a question of the historical evidence: but whether it might fitly be so. I am not trying to prove that it must necessarily have been so, in order that the fatal link of hereditary sin might be broken: I feel no satisfaction in arguments of this kind. I am asking, I repeat, whether it might fitly be so; whether such a miracle would be appropriate to such an occasion? And I reply that, so far as I am capable of judging, if miracle be admitted at all, this is a point at which it might reasonably and appropriately come in. The infinite significance of the moment might fitly be signalised by miracle.

My argument is a long one, and perhaps to

some minds a difficult one. Let me briefly state its chief heads up to this point.

The Incarnation—that is, the coming of the Son of God in human flesh—was prepared for by the teaching of the Old Testament as to the original constitution of man in the Divine image. This teaching witnessed to a certain kinship between man and God, and so to the fitness of humanity for union with Deity.

In the earliest Gospel story we have a picture of a human life more perfect than ever we could have conceived for ourselves: a life which our deepest instincts tell us is the most God-like thing that has ever been seen: a life which presents an insoluble mystery, if He who lived it was not more than man; for He made both promises and claims which are inconceivable in a good man who was no more than a man: a life which admits of one explanation only, namely, that it was—as it was believed to be—the incarnate life of the Son of God.

We saw further that this life was full of miracle, and of appropriate miracle: of miracle that was a fit exponent of a new life-power manifesting itself in the world.

We then asked whether it would be appropriate

that such a life should be ushered on to the stage of history by a miraculous beginning? Whether this would not be in harmony with its miraculous course and its miraculous sequel? And I answered for myself, that in my judgment, if miracle were admitted at all, this was a point at which miracle might appropriately come in.

That it would be appropriate at this point does not, of course, prove that it actually took place. But it sets our minds free to consider without bias the historical evidence which supports the miracle: and on this subject I shall have something to say next time.

Meanwhile let us bow in adoration of Him who has made us for Himself, who has lifted us out of our fall, who has 'so loved the world that He gave His only-begotten Son' to be incarnate and made man for us men and our salvation. Brothers, how sacred is our manhood since God has taken it to Himself in Jesus Christ!

III

The point which we reached at the close of the last lecture was this: If the Incarnation of the Son of God be accepted as true; if indeed He came down from heaven and was incarnate and was made man; if the whole story of His life is full of miracle, and of miracle which is always appropriate to its purpose of declaring the new power which had entered into human life: then it would not appear to be inappropriate that this incarnate life should be marked at the outset by a signal miracle. As a matter of fact the two only records which we possess of the circumstances of our Lord's birth agree in describing it as a miraculous birth from a Virgin Mother.

It is exceedingly easy for those who approach the matter from a different side to discredit the accounts of the miraculous birth which are contained in our first and third Gospels. Let me give you an example of the way in which this has lately been done. A recent critic writing for English readers says: 'When one compares the two narratives together, one finds not only that they come from different sources, but that they are inconsistent one with the other.' He proceeds to disparage the first narrative on account of the story of the Star which follows it, and the second on account of an apparent error in chronology. Each writer is shown to be untrustworthy in certain particulars: their credit as witnesses is thus undermined.

It is really astonishing that language of this kind should be used by persons who in other departments have done valuable historical work, and who claim a hearing on the ground of their acquaintance with historical method. That the narratives come from different sources is provable only in one way: namely, by their apparent inconsistency of statement. That they are inconsistent one with the other, and that they come from different sources, are surely not two counts in the indictment: at most they are an observation and a conclusion based on the observation.

Moreover, that an event is attested by two stories coming from different sources is usually regarded as affording a presumption of truth, not of falsehood. When two narratives differ in certain points of detail, and yet agree in the main topic which they undertake to set forth, historical criticism usually regards the point of agreement as having the stronger claim on our acceptance, just because of the divergence in the accessory details.

Indeed this contrast between the two stories is the first point to which I should myself desire to direct your attention. We have, as a matter of fact, two notably different narratives of the Virgin-birth. One is shown by internal evidence to come from the pen of a devout Jew, who is firmly convinced of the Messiahship of Jesus, and eager to find Old Testament parallels to all the events of His earthly history. Thus, when he has mentioned a number of miraculous cures, such as he found recorded in St Mark's Gospel and copied thence into his own book, he adds the words of the prophet Isaiah, as though they were the very ground for the working of these miracles: 'In order that it might be fulfilled which was spoken through Isaiah the prophet: He took our infirmities Himself and carried our diseases.' That shows you the type of mind of this writer. He is always seeking a sanction for the event which has come to his knowledge, and his sanction often seems to us to be fetched from far. Yet we feel that he has a reverence for truth, which finds expression in a way that appealed to his fellow-countrymen, if it does not equally appeal to all of us.

The other narrative comes from a writer of a wholly different temperament and of quite other antecedents. He is not a Jew of Palestine, if he is a Jew at all. He is a writer who is familiar with Greek literature and Greek modes of thought. He professes to have made careful enquiries in order that he may write accurate history. Where we can test him, as in the Acts of the Apostles, by such historical evidence as inscriptions afford, we find him astonishingly exact in minute details. We discover that he was an unusually careful observer; and at this we are the less surprised when we learn incidentally that he was a medical man: for then, as now, the practice of medicine trained the faculty of observation and promoted a reverence for fact.

Each of these writers, then, has a reverential mind, which encourages us to believe that he would not record anything of which he was not profoundly convinced. The second of them appeals to us of to-day with by far the greater force. To speak of historical and scientific method in regard to a writer in ancient times would be an anachronism : but, if habitual accuracy of observation be a recommendation in an author of any period, we may indeed be thankful that in the case of this particular miracle we are not without the testimony of the one writer of the New Testament who most clearly displays the historical instinct, 'Luke, the beloved physician.'

I would next ask you to notice the remarkable way in which these two writers undesignedly supplement each other's account. There is not the least reason for thinking that either had seen the work of the other: if he had, he must almost of necessity have endeavoured to bring his own narrative into greater harmony with it.

Now, presuming that the event which they both record really happened, we can see that two persons must have been impressed by it in a way that would leave a permanent mark on their recital of the story. The husband to whom the Virgin was betrothed would be thrown into the most painful perplexity. As a pious Jew he would be in an agony as to the right and religious course to adopt. On the other hand, the betrothed Virgin must of necessity have been prepared in advance by some special revelation; and to accept such a revelation would require an act of extraordinary faith.

It is surely a noteworthy coincidence that, whereas we have only two narratives of the events, and whereas the two writers have obviously no conscious intention of supplementing each other, they do, as a matter of fact, answer the very questions which our instincts require to have answered. One shows us Joseph's anxiety and the Divine admonition by which it was relieved. The other tells of Mary's simple faith, which accepts the angelic announcement when it is enforced by the reminder that 'nothing is too hard for God.'

There were two persons only who could offer valid testimony as to the wonderful event; two ultimate sources only of trustworthy information. It is no small satisfaction to be assured that neither source of information fails us, and that our two independent narratives represent respectively the story as told from the standpoint of St Joseph and the story as told from the standpoint of the Blessed Virgin herself.

Let us again, for the sake of clearness, resume the heads of our argument. We saw last time that, if the Son of God indeed entered into our human life, a miraculous mode of entry might well be regarded as appropriate. We have seen to-day that we have two independent records which describe such a miraculous entry: that they come from writers of very different habits and temperaments: that, while the surrounding details differ so much that to our limited knowledge they present an appearance of inconsistency, yet they are absolutely in agreement on the central and essential matter of the Virgin-birth, and that they tell the story as we should most have wished to have it told, from the two points of view of St Joseph and St Mary.

Of course, this is not by itself complete historical proof; it is not offered as such. But if anything can lend credibility to an event of this nature it is the simplicity and the supplementary character of the only two narratives of it which we possess.

It may be well in passing to emphasise the fact that we have no other narrative at all which is independent of these two. The apocryphal Gospels are sometimes referred to as if they discredited the canonical Gospels. I could wish that these apocryphal Gospels were half as much read as they are alluded to. Those of us who have most carefully investigated them know that they are not independent of our Gospels, that they pander to a curiosity for information as to points on which our Gospels are silent, and that the study of them sends us back to our Gospels with the profoundest reassurance. The frigid miracle-mongering of the so-called Gospels of the Infancy, when compared with the transparent honesty and the delicate reserve of our evangelists, offers one of the most instructive contrasts in all literature.

It is impossible in such a lecture as this to present that part of the evidence for the early belief in the Virgin-birth which is to be collected from primitive Church writers. I refer you to a little book on the Apostles' Creed, published by Dr. Swete, which gives an admirable and accurate summary.[1] I may add a quotation from the adverse critic whom I quoted at the outset: 'The story of the Virgin-birth was certainly widely spread in the Church before the end of the first century.'

[1] *The Apostles' Creed: Its Relation to Primitive Christianity*, by Professor Swete. (London: C. J. Clay & Sons, Ave Maria Lane.)

Let us return to consider the general character of our evidence. The earliest of our Gospels was written about 60 years after the birth of Christ. St Mark had no occasion to refer to this matter, for he begins his story 30 years later, at the Baptism of John. There is nothing to show whether he knew of the miracle or did not know of it; and it is quite idle to speculate on this point. About ten years later St Luke wrote his account, the nature of which suggests that his information came ultimately from the Blessed Virgin. I see no reason for thinking that he used any pre-existing document at this point: he was probably putting the story into writing for the first time, as the result of his own enquiries; and his style is modelled on the old Hebrew stories which he was familiar with through the Greek translation of the Old Testament. St Matthew's Gospel was written, I think, later. The account there given appears to be derived ultimately from St Joseph.

This is the natural explanation of the existence of these two accounts. If there were no miraculous element involved, this would be regarded as unusually good historical evidence. The story is told from the points of view of the two persons chiefly concerned. Neither writer knows of the narrative of the other, and, as we might expect, the surrounding details are very divergent. But the central event is a matter of complete agreement between them. Therefore in an ordinary case we should say that, whatever uncertainty attached to these details, the divergence only strengthened the certainty of the matter of agreement.

On the testimony of these two narratives, supported possibly by a tradition preserved in the circle of the descendants of our Lord's brethren, early writers like Ignatius accepted the miracle; it found a mention in the Creed which gradually shaped itself in the second century; and it retained its place both in the Eastern and Western forms of that Creed.

If this miracle never took place at all, two serious problems confront us.

(1) The first is a problem of literary criticism. How are we to account for the words 'Virgin Mary' in the second century Creed? How are we to account for such a sentence as that of Ignatius in A.D. 110? 'Hidden from the prince of this world were the virginity of Mary and her child-bearing, and likewise also the death of the Lord—three mysteries to be cried aloud, which

were wrought in the silence of God.' It is a passing allusion : but how are we to explain its occurrence ?

The only reasonable literary explanation is that the early Church accepted the Gospel narratives as true. But then, what of those narratives themselves, if the thing never happened? How did they come to be? Were the two evangelists deceived? for no one will now allege that they were conscious deceivers. And if so, how were they deceived? Can a myth have grown up and have gained such currency as to deceive St Luke within forty years of the death of Christ? You must give the story time to develop into the two striking narratives which we possess: you must put it back to a date at which probably the Virgin was still living: and you must further find a ground for its origination.

There appears to be no doctrinal ground for its invention in these early times. St Luke was a follower of St Paul; but St Paul never bases the Incarnation upon it—indeed, never so much as mentions it. And neither St Matthew nor St Luke puts it to any doctrinal purpose.

It has been suggested that legends of parthenogenesis are found in heathen mythology; and the story of Buddha is given as an example of the growth of such a legend. But the whole atmosphere of the Judaism of the time appears to me to be unfavourable to the transplantation of heathen myths. And if there is one characteristic of the first Christian teaching, it is the proclamation of *truth*. The shadows of superstition are scattered: figments are thrust aside on every hand: 'children of light,' 'children of day'—these are the epithets of new converts. Where are we to find the dark corners in which these new superstitions grew? And even if they did grow in some obscure place, was St Luke the writer who was likely to be imposed upon by them?

I cannot myself accept a tissue of improbabilities as affording a reasonable account of these early narratives. If I felt absolutely precluded from believing in the possibility of the miracle of the Virgin-birth, I should find myself faced by a literary problem utterly insoluble by any intelligible process. I could not account for the origin of these narratives, nor for the acceptance of the Virgin-birth by the early Christians.

(2) A second problem faces me when I con-

sider the situation, not now as a literary critic, but as a member of the Christian Church. I believe that the Church is the Body of Christ and one with Himself. I believe that it is His representative in the world, the instrument of His working, the witness of His truth. I believe that the doctrine of His Incarnation is the central teaching of Christianity and the peculiar treasure entrusted to the keeping of His Church. I believe that the Holy Spirit is promised to guide the Church into the truth about Christ.

How then can I explain the witness of the Church to the Virgin-birth, given in her briefest Creed, proclaimed by all her great theologians, reverently cherished by her simplest saints, if after all it is a figment of superstitious imagination? Has she unconsciously repeated a lie at every baptism since her baptismal Creed took shape—i.e. at least from the middle of the second century to the present day? She with her mission of truth which dispersed the black night of the heathen religions, driving them off the face of the earth because they were false?

I have no answer to such questions as these. I can conceive of no adequate reason why the Church should have been permitted to include this miracle among the sacred mysteries of the Creed, if it never took place—if the Virgin Mary were not the Virgin after all.

I have kept this consideration apart. I have treated the literary problem by itself. But the one difficulty is reinforced by the other difficulty, and the two together effectually bar the way for me. They make it impossible for me to explain the story of the Virgin-birth as a legend of the pious imagination of the first generation after the crucifixion of our Lord.

I know that there may be some who will not feel as I feel that, in view of the literary history, and in view of the history of the Christian Church throughout the ages, it is easier to believe than to disbelieve this special miracle. But those who have followed the whole of my argument will at least understand that, if the possibility of miracle be admitted at all, a belief in the Virgin-birth is not inconsistent with loyalty to the principles of literary and historical research, and that it cannot be dismissed off-hand as a relic of primitive superstition.

But, as I said at the outset, it is the wonder of the Incarnation itself, and not the wonder of the mode of its manifestation, that I desire to commend to your special attention. It is more wonderful that the Son of God should come down from heaven and be incarnate and made man, than that His incarnate life should have begun with a Virgin-birth. Let us fix our faith on the greater wonder, and seek to understand how much it has wrought for the exaltation of the humanity which Christ has taken to Himself. I had hoped that I might have been able to have treated this last point at some length. But our time has been occupied, not unprofitably, I hope, with matters which seemed to press at this particular moment. I can, therefore, only indicate briefly a few thoughts for your own further study.

First, in the light of the Incarnation, we see a glorious destiny for the human race. These are days in which the most earnest minds look away from the problem of their own individual future, and are fascinated by the larger consideration of the purpose which God has with the world of men. Humanity as a whole must, we feel, have a meaning and destiny. The reason why Tennyson appeals to many of us in a way that Browning never can is that, while Browning is interested in the perfecting of the individual, Tennyson looks to the perfecting of the race. To quote one illustration from a poem of his later years, entitled 'The Making of Man':

All about him shadow still, but, while the races
flower and fade,
Prophet-eyes can catch a glory slowly gaining on
the shade,
Till the peoples all are one, and all their voices join
in choric
Hallelujah to the Maker, 'It is finish'd. Man is
made.'

It is this conception of the unity and solidarity of mankind that is specially illuminated by the Incarnation. Christ took man upon Him. He united Himself with humanity; not with the fortunes of a chosen race, as the Jews had fancied, but with the destiny of the whole of mankind. He came 'that the world through Him might be saved.' He showed that the true human life was the life of self-giving, not self-saving. He took our humanity on to His cross. He took it through the grave and gate of death to a joyful resurrection. He took it up to the throne of God. And thereby He endowed it with an immortal hope.

But again, He asserted the sacredness of that humanity which was thus capable of union with

God. He claimed the whole of our common human life. No factor in its progress is excluded from His claim. All that is truly human is consecrated by the Incarnation. The human body has gained a new sacredness, since 'the Word became flesh.' All life is seen to be sacred, because Christ lived a human life. Every highest faculty, every noblest achievement, is a crown to be cast at length at the feet of the Christ. Need I urge this thought in a place which has gathered to itself in holy consecration the memorials of every form of service which man has rendered to his fellow-man?

Lastly, each individual life has gained a measure of ennoblement to the eye of faith by the Incarnation of the Son of God as Man. How can we despise any the least or any the most fallen of these sons of men whose human nature Christ has shared? He has claimed them each and all. They are 'brothers for whom Christ died.' We may not despair of one of them. We may not despair of ourselves. Utterly unworthy though we be, He beckons us along His own pathway. He says, 'I know you: I know what is in man: his weakness and his strength: his temptations, and his capacity to rise above them in union with the Divine. You need never despair. Rise and follow Me. Go and sin no more.' He has made Himself one with us, in order that we may find a new strength in Him. He calls us to be consciously one with Him : and His call is our hope.